Contents

The dinosaurs

Dinosaurs were reptiles.

Dinosaurs lived long ago.

Tyrannosaurus rex was a dinosaur.
Tyrannosaurus rex lived long ago.

Today there are no
Tyrannosaurus rex.

Tyrannosaurus rex

Velociraptor

Some dinosaurs were small.

But Tyrannosaurus rex was big.

Tyrannosaurus rex had strong
back legs.

Tyrannosaurus rex walked on
two feet.

Tyrannosaurus rex had short arms.

Tyrannosaurus rex had a long tail.

Tyrannosaurus rex had sharp teeth.

Tyrannosaurus rex had
strong jaws.

Tyrannosaurus rex had a very big head.

Tyrannosaurus rex ate
other dinosaurs.

How do we know?

Scientists have found fossils
of Tyrannosaurus rex.

Fossils are the bones of animals which have turned to rock.

fossil

Fossils show us the outline
of the dinosaur.

Fossils tell us what Tyrannosaurus rex was like.

Fossil quiz

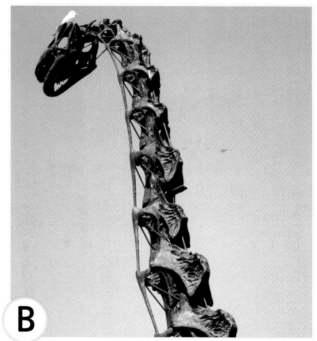

One of these fossils was Tyrannosaurus rex. Can you tell which one?

Picture glossary

dinosaur a reptile who lived millions of years ago

fossil part of a dead plant or animal that has become hard like rock

reptile a cold-blooded animal

Answer to question on page 22
Fossil A was Tyrannosaurus rex.
Fossil B was Brachiosaurus.

Index

Note to Parents and Teachers
Before reading
Talk to the children about dinosaurs. Do they know the names of any dinosaurs? What features did they have e.g. long neck, bony plates, sharp teeth? Has anyone seen a dinosaur fossil or model in a museum?

After reading
- Dinosaur footprints
  Outside draw large dinosaur footprints in playground chalks. Tell the children to move around the footprints using different dinosaur movements. When you call out "Stop" also call out a number. The children should have to quickly stand in groups of that number on the footprints.
- Make a Tyrannosaurus head
  Give each child a lump of clay. Show them the pictures of Tyrannosaurus head and ask them to make a model head from the clay. When it is dry they could paint the head, colouring some of the teeth red to represent the blood of the animal it has attacked.
- Dinosaur poem.
  Ask the children to suggest some descriptions of the dinosaurs and link these together to make a simple poem e.g. Hungry dinosaurs, Hunting dinosaurs, Down in the swamp.